Prai

*The Skiers Gift Book that's Sweeping the ...*
*(Sort of)*

"Insightful and entertaining!"     - Maria R.

"It was a one sit read. I loved it!"     - Shirley A.

"My wife got tired of my reading the funny parts to her. Leave it to Dan Cody who had me laughing so hard I may have experienced skigasm in my own home. A fast read that is hilarious and yet insightful about the things you need to know most about skiing. It'd be a great gift for any skier or wannabe."
                                        - Bob R.

"Good solid information with a touch of sarcasm. A good fun book to psyche you up for skiing. Read it."
                                        - Ski it up

"Hilarious! I wish I would have known earlier about the laws of comfortable boots, types of skis, warmest outerwear, and that when choosing ski resorts, size matters! Ha! It's a laugh out read and perfect for the dedicated skier in your life. Thank you Dan Cody!!!"                   - Snow bunny

# The Skiers Gift Book That's Sweeping the Globe
# (Sort Of)

## Second Edition

Dan Cody

ISBN-13: 978-0-578-57770-8

Some characters and events in this book are fictitious. Any similarity to real
persons, living or dead, is coincidental and not intended by the author.

Books may be purchased by contacting the publisher:
Whyze Group, Inc.
2233 S. Overlook Rd.
Cleveland, Ohio, USA 44106
jason@whyzegroup.com

# DEDICATION

To my expedition partner, inspirer, confidant, best friend, lover and joy, OP.

.

# CONTENTS

# DAN CODY

# ACKNOWLEDGMENTS

It takes the discerning eyes, generosity and honest feedback of friends to turn a book draft into something more. Thanks goes to Maria Ross, Roy Katz, Bob Rosenbaum and Shirley Angelo for their reviews and suggestions on the first edition. For help on the section about skis, thanks go to my friends at newschoolers.com, Matt, abar, BigPurpleSkiSuit, OregonDead, father q, TRVP_ANGEL, Casey, and Jason Bledsoe. For help with the cover design, thanks to Mitch Olman, Bob Rosenbaum, Jim Wright and Dr. Peg. Just so you know, I could have done this without you—but it would have sucked. Thank you.

# 1
# INTRODUCTION:
# WHY SKIERKIND NEEDED THIS BOOK

Since its original publication in 2017, *The Skiers Gift Book That's Sweeping the Globe (Sort Of)* has provided ski industry insider tips and laughs to skiers, snowboarders and skier-wannabes in seven countries. It's also become an Amazon best-seller.

Ok, maybe being the 1.6 millionth best-selling book on Amazon doesn't earn best seller status in your world. But in my world, there are 48.5 million Amazon books. This book's being the 1.6 millionth best seller makes my book a better seller than 96% of the books on Amazon.

This is my way of reassuring you that the journey we'll walk together in these pages has been validated by those who have come before you and given it five-star Amazon ratings. We will experience truth, adventure and a few belly laughs on the way to the slopes.

This book has something for everyone; skiers and those considering trying skiing or snowboarding for the first time. Skiers will relate to the comic lengths we go through to follow our passions—passions that lead us to icy mountain roads, sub-zero temperatures and onto remote high-altitude peaks in the "death zone". This is what we do for *fun*.

Skiers are ample inspiration for strange and often hilarious stories that I use to inform, entertain and help get you stoked for your next ski holiday.

If you're considering trying skiing or snowboarding for the first time, I'll give you all the insider secrets that you need to get started happily and affordably.

Why's this important?

Most people who try skiing for the first time go with a friend or family member who skis. No surprise. But, the next tidbit may surprise you.

How many people return to a ski resort after their first visit? Ninety percent? Seventy-five percent? If you're a skier or snowboarder, you'll be bummed to hear it's fewer.

We skiers and boarders have a hard time imagining anyone *quitting* after their first day on the slopes. We love our sports. We love talking about them almost as much as doing them. We get excited about sliding down mountains, spectacular scenery and good times with family and friends. We read books about this stuff. We drool over cool snowboarding and skiing videos.

But, most of us have forgotten what it's like to be a beginner. That's one reason why the number of skiers hasn't kept up with population growth.

A couple of years ago, I looked into this. I researched the global ski industry, including reading through hundred-page reports by Snowsports Industry America. I eventually found the number I was looking for—the number of first time skiers who return to ski again.

Ready? The number is…drumroll…sixteen percent. Only one in six people who try skiing returns to a ski resort. Ever.

Now, if you're considering trying skiing or boarding for the first time, *don't let this discourage you!* I, your knowledgeable Sherpa, will guide you to the mountains where you'll enjoy an awesome time. Stick with me here.

We'll do a few important things that will make your first experience on the slopes so enjoyable that you can't wait to go back! This is a big reason why I wrote this book.

In addition to providing a few laughs, *The Skiers Gift Book that's Sweeping the Globe (Sort of)* assures that your first skiing or snowboarding experiences are affordable, comfortable, convenient and fun from day one. You'll want to do it again and again. Trust me.

Before we go further, I have to acknowledge a gap in this book. This gap is created by the title of this book, which includes the words, *Sweeping the Globe.*

You see, modern skiing was invented in Norway. So, the idea that anyone in Norway would take seriously a book about skiing written by an American—me—is a stretch. It would be like a baseball book titled, "Ultimate Baseball" by Torrill Kvitvenfeld, a writer who lives in Humptulips. Yes, there really is a village named Humptulips, and no, few American baseball fans would buy his book.

In fact, skiing is a global sport. It's more popular in other regions like the Alps for example than in the U.S. And, any book on skiing that doesn't address the sport at length in Europe, Asia, New Zealand and South America is less than perfect. Hence, this is a work in progress, improved each year by the suggestions of skiers worldwide.

That said, this book, this journey, will change your life.

So, don your boots fellow traveler. We begin...

# 2

# TRUST ME. REALLY

At this point, you may be wondering, "What makes you, Dan, a reputable guide on this journey to this high altitude, sub-zero zone of fulfillment?"

Your concerns are well-taken.

After all, we're talking about your vacation days—you know, the days off you've accumulated at work but which your Scrooge-of-a-boss won't let you use (in America anyway. Bosses in other countries are more enlightened about holiday time). We're also talking about your hard-earned vacation money and your enjoyment of life in general.

So, let's get down to why you should trust my advice here.

I've worked in most aspects of the ski industry. I was a certified instructor and taught hundreds of people how to ski at east and west coast resorts in the U.S. I've observed thousands of skiers at dozens of ski resorts. I've worked in sales and marketing at ski resorts, managed resort hotels, sold ski equipment and chaperoned ski bus tours. And, it all started with my first job as a pot washer at Killington, Vermont, USA.

So, I've been in positions from which I could observe skiers who were experiencing great ski vacations and others who were cold and frustrated. I share my observations and conclusions and have invited book reviews from skiers worldwide for two years. So far, the reviews have been 99% "thumbs up."

The chapters on teaching yourself and others how to ski are informed mostly by my experiences teaching skiing at Greek Peak in New York and Heavenly Ski Resort, California, USA. I learned to teach skiing by using metaphors. Metaphors have emerged in brain science as an important means by which we simplify complex experiences—like how to ride slippery boards down snowy mountains.

So, as a complement to ski lessons you'll get at ski resorts, I run dry land workshops that rely on metaphors to aid in skiing moguls, steeps, powder and hard pack. In case you're interested, that program is a multi-media infotainment event—one that mixes videos, dancing, drinks and beach chairs. Really edgy stuff. You'd like it. Drop me a line at dancodyauthor@gmail.com to get more info about this.

Anyway, back to the book and why you should trust my advice here.

I'm really passionate about skiing. I'm passionate about helping *you* enjoy skiing, snowboarding or both. We skiers are fanatics about this beautiful sport. We've not always done a great job of showing our friends how to take up the sport themselves.

Part of the challenge is that we've had to rely on small ski businesses for guidance about where to ski and what to buy. The marketing budgets of most ski resorts and equipment manufacturers are tiny compared to those of household brands like Google or McDonalds. Ski businesses have just enough marketing dollars to show us happy skiers using their products and not much more.

Over the years, I've found that ski businesses couldn't always provide the help I really needed. When I was a beginner, I remember wondering, "How do I start skiing?" Should I go to a ski resort and watch other people? How do I dress warmly enough on my first ski trip without expensive ski wear?

As I became more experienced, my questions changed. What's a good-fitting ski boot supposed to feel like on my foot? (This literally took years and least two ill-fitting pairs of ski boots to figure out.) When should I stop renting ski equipment and buy my own? How do I figure out which skis to buy? Does looking at their graphics help? How do I carry all this equipment? Which ski resorts will I enjoy the most? Where should I stay overnight? How do I find discounts on lift passes, skis, transportation and lodging? And the granddaddy of all questions, how do I become a better skier?

It wasn't until years later, after I had worked at several ski resorts and talked with dozens of ski professionals that I had the answers to all of most questions.

Let me repeat that. I literally had to leave my friends, family and a steady paycheck to move to the mountains to get the answers. If you're like most recreational skiers, that's…well…crazy.

My mission is to help you avoid quitting school, or your job, and leaving your family to go into the mountains to become a ski bum to learn the answers to skiing's deepest mysteries.

So, continue on this journey with me, my friend, but don't expect any cheap thrills. These are hard-earned thrills. I share them with you as my most substantive contribution to skierkind.

*The Skiers Gift Book That's Sweeping the Globe (Sort Of) Second Edition* gives skiers and skier wannabes an insider's view on how to start skiing, keep skiing happily, save money, and does it in a way that most readers find valuable and fun.

Skiing at any level of proficiency is great when you also feel confident about how you're using your precious vacation time and money. That's what this book is about.

Skiing and snowboarding feel magical. Just ask any skier or snowboarder. Amazing, super-exciting, fun and stoked are words you're bound to here.

In no other sport do you have the same ability to control what I've described as the world's best rollercoaster ride. You can go as fast or slow as you want. You can turn as sharply or as gently as you wish. You can slide around blissfully or carve deep turns with 3 Gs of force. You can feel the compression of knolls and the weightlessness of dips.

And, you can do it all with your friends, economically and happily, in the most spectacular scenery on the planet.

This is how you achieve winter time *nirvana*. Ready?

# 3

# FOUR SIGNS OF SKIER ECSTASY

Depending on where skiers are and what they're doing, there are telltale signs of skiers ecstasy:

*At the Base Lodge*

You can see this as skiers return from their morning or afternoon escapades on the hill. As they re-enter the lodge, they will lift their goggles and lock eyes with each other. They'll exclaim to the disruption of moms and little children nearby, "That was AMAZING!" They may even look for a cigarette. This is where stock brokers and systems analysts abandon all discretion.

*On the Mountain, Midway to End of a Run*

This is where most of the action happens. The most obvious sign of skier ecstasy is heard from the lift as you pass overhead. It's the loud "Woooo hooo" that gives it away. These are made by skiers in the throes of passion. These may be accompanied by one fist-bump or repeated fist-bumps for those who still have something left at the bottom of the run.

If it's a deep powder day, there may be another sign of rapture on the hill that's less obvious. You'll have to look closely at the faces of skiers as they descend. Watch for the crescent of snow that's caked up against their smiley face underneath.

*On the Mountain, at the Top of a Run*

Celebrations at the top of the mountain are spotted more rarely than those in the base lodge or midway down the piste. But, they're probably spotted more frequently than Bigfoot. So, get your video app ready.

This is where skiers stand at the top of run, writhing as if making out with the entire valley below. Top-of-mountain moments of ecstasy are best recorded on sunny days but frequently happen during heavy snow storms when gobs of champagne powder are falling.

*In the Terrain Park*

The terrain park is where most of the grinding happens at a ski resort. The good news is that almost everyone keeps their pants on. Most grinding happens between the bottom of one's skis and the resort's surplus plumbing, lumber and cars, which have been creatively strewn across the slope.

As if the flotsam in the snow weren't enough, there are also jumps, half pipes and kickers over which daredevils fly.

The stakes are high as skiers grind their way down pipes, rails, stairs, walls and launch themselves skyward...which is the easy part. The hard part is landing in the same state of health as one took off.

Surviving a run in the park is ample cause for fist bumps. And, regardless of whether your move ends with landing on your feet or your face, as long as it's spectacular, you'll have provided worthy entertainment for your fellow skiers, too.

# 4

# SKI HOLIDAY BUZZKILLS AND HOW TO AVOID THEM

Skiing is a sensual sport. You'll feel yourself gliding across the snow, the crisp air against your cheeks, the sun at your back. The only sounds you'll here will be those of your skis, the wind, and your heart pounding with excitement.

It's easy to get in the mood for this stuff. And, setting the mood requires knowing what the potential buzzkills to ski holidays are and how to avoid them. Skiing and snowboarding should be affordable, comfortable, convenient and most of all, *fun*.

That's what this book is about, especially the fun parts. And, this is so worthy of remembering that this is the shortest chapter with one of the longest chapter titles.

# 5

# SKIING WITH THE VILLAGE IDIOT?

Here the seeds of disaster are sewn long before you ever get to the resort. The people you ski with can make or break your skiing experience. Fortunately, skiers are generally a pretty affable bunch. This is due to our temperament.

You've got to be a little loosey-goosey upstairs to hurl down a mountain on a pair of sticks wearing little protection other than a brain bucket. This is part of our charm. Our lack of sufficient fear to assure survival accounts for our sociability, too. We're not afraid to start conversations with perfect strangers on lift rides, in the base lodge, wherever.

Nonetheless, there are some skiers whom you should cross off your prospective ski buddy list. These include anyone you or your current ski buddies haven't known for at least a year. This year-long hazing is the best litmus test I know for assuring you'll have a good time. And, not coincidentally, this is how I have been screened by others before being invited to go on several memorable ski holidays.

You might be thinking that this year-long screening is overkill. But, when you consider that you're going to be spending your precious vacation time and money, you better make sure that you haven't unwittingly invited a ski holiday thug who will ruin your ski vacation.

The exception to this rule is when you've signed up for a ski club trip. In this case, you'll have little control of who else goes with you. This is usually fine as there's typically enough people on club trips to find friends and a suitable subgroup with whom you can ski. If you're married someone who skis near your ability, then club trips are a breeze.

If you're single, beware and be prepared to take steps. Unless you do, you may be roomed with the club's village idiot. Every club has one. Try to find out if that's the case before your room arrangements are finalized. If necessary, find another roommate, or upgrade to a single room or go on a different ski trip.

Do not attempt to room with the village idiot if you can help it. You'll spend your entire ski holiday trying to avoid them. They'll suck the life out of you. Instead of coming home at the end of your vacation refreshed and happy, you'll return a shriveled shell with dark circles who wants nothing more than to curl up on the floor of your own shower.

# 6

# 7 WAYS TO SPOT THE PERFECT SKI BOOTS FOR YOU

Repeat after me…

"Comfortable ski boots are the most important thing."

"Comfortable ski boots are the most important thing."

"Comfortable ski boots are THE MOST IMPORTANT THING!"

Bad ski boots prevent skier ecstasy.

Even if you're forced to room with Hannibal Lector on your next ski trip, you can't escape if you can't ski because your boots hurt. Ski boots are supposed to be snug enough to transfer lower leg movements to your skis. They are not supposed to hurt or cut off blood flow to your feet.

There's a lot of mythology around what ski boots to buy, how they're supposed to fit and even how to put ski boots on.

So, here are a few pointers.

If you're going skiing for the first time, rent boots and skis. There's no point investing in hardware this early in the game. Go skiing a few times and get your feet under you. You've got time to figure out whether you want to buy boots and how they should feel when they fit correctly. By the way, if you're going to buy hardware, start with a comfortable pair of ski boots.

Unless you have significant skiing experience or aggressively ski any terrain in any snow conditions, you are very likely a candidate for a low- to mid-priced ski boot. These are in the $200 to $500 US range, with a few exceptions. Generally, boots in this price range are comfortably padded inside and are stiff enough to transfer leg movements to the ski. They're perfect for most recreational skiers.

If you are an experienced, aggressive skier who can verbalize what "high performance" means to you, then you'll probably be interested in boots that are $400 to $750 US or more.

This is where boot lingo departs from that used by most recreational skiers. If you know ski boot words like "stiffness," "forward lean," "canting," "cuff angle" and "lateral stiffness" mean, you'll have a better chance of making good investments in high performance ski boots. Of course, you may not want to blow seven hundred bucks on a pair of ski boots, and that's OK. Your ten-year-old pair of recreational ski boots is working just fine, thank you.

But, there might be times when you just want to impress your significant other or ski shop sales people with your worldly knowledge. So, here's a short introduction to seven dimensions of ski boot design :

*Stiffness* – Ski boot stiffness refers to the flexibility of the boot's outer shell. A softer shell reduces the transmission of skiers' leg movements to their skis. This is an advantage for new skiers, who tend to over correct. A beginner skier who's skiing in high performance boots would be like driving a car on ice while snapping the steering wheel left and right.

Expert skiers and racers use stiffer boots to transmit subtler leg movements to the ski. But, some experts, particularly freestyle skiers, prefer a softer flexing shell. When skiing aggressively in the bumps, a softer shell transmits less shock from the skis to the lower legs and saves the shins and knees from wear and tear. But, keep in mind that stiffness refers to the material used for the entire shell. You can sometimes find a laterally stiff boot than allows for a lot of fore-aft flex at the ankle.

*Lateral stiffness* – This refers to the boot's ability to tilt the ski on its edge without the boot flexing in the side-to-side plane. This is more important today than in skiing's dark ages, when overall boot stiffness mattered more. Back in the 1960s, ski boot manufacturers transitioned from leather lace up boots to plastic boots with buckles. The plastic could be made stiffer than leather and could be molded to create a cuff that rose higher on the shin. This gave skiers more leverage and control of their skis than leather did.

But, as I said, this was the end of the dark ages of ski technology and the beginnings of its renaissance. In cold weather, plastic boots were, and still are, prone to adopting the flex characteristics of concrete. Whereas, during a day of skiing, leather boots took on more of a cold, squishy-but-form-fitting shape, plastic boots are unyielding. Some experienced skiers developed painful sore spots on their feet and shins. New skiers gave up the sport out of the agony they experienced during their first days in ski boots.

Today however, there are ski boots that are laterally stiff while the forward flex remains soft. These may not work well if you're a serious racer. But, if you're skiing all over the mountain, on groomed slopes, in the bumps and through the crud, then these boots might give you the control and the flexibility you want out of a good all mountain ski boot.

*Forward lean* – This refers to the angle of your ankle or, more accurately, at the boot's ankle. Depending on how much bend there is, you'll need to bend your knees to compensate, bringing your center of gravity over your feet. Or, in non-technical terms, putting your keister over your feet, not in front of them.

So, a day of skiing in high performance boots is going to be more tiring because your ankles and knees are bent more than in a recreational ski boot. Generally speaking, recreational ski boots allow you to stand up straighter, making standing in lift lines and skiing less exhausting.

*Cuff angle* – If you were to look at your boots from the back, this is the angle created by the heel cup of the boot and the cuff that rises above the heel cup and closes around your shin. Normally, this angle is zero, but sometimes an adjustment is needed to compensate if your shin bone is unusually curved or you're bow-legged or knock-kneed.

*Cant* – This refers to the tilt of your ski when you stand in a normal straight skiing position with equal weight on both boots and bindings. If you're standing with your skis at a comfortable skiing distance from each other, say hip width, you might find that an edge of one or both skis is pressed more deeply into the snow than the other edge. This is likely to make turning to one side harder. Canting wedges will help you achieve a neutral ski-to-snow orientation. This mean that, when you're making turns while skiing, you'll be able to roll both skis onto their edges at the same time, to the same degree.

*Boot fitter* – You may need the help of a boot fitting pro to customize your ski boot's fit around each foot. There are a couple of reasons why this might be the case.

One reason is that you may have atypical feet. The shapes of your left and right feet may be different. Or, you could have bunions or bursars, for example. Few of us have perfect feet. In most cases, a boot fitter can stretch your boot's shell and adjust padding where necessary to make you perfectly comfortable.

*Padding* – A second reason for using a boot fitter is you may want to get a better fit in your high performance boots. These boots forego about half the padding of a mid-priced recreational ski boot. Right away, this should strike you as a potential risk akin to medieval torture.

High performance boots are designed to provide a closer, more responsive fit. That implies that, without that extra padding in the liner, there's a greater chance that the boot will be uncomfortable unless it's form fitted to each of your feet. That's where all the bells and whistles on these boots come in.

Getting a proper fit may require a couple of visits to your boot fitter, who will greet you enthusiastically if you bring her beer and cash.

# 7

# 2 SCIENTIFIC SECRETS OF PUTTING ON COMFORTABLE SKI BOOTS

This might seem like regression to your childhood when you learned how to dress yourself—or at least your parents tried to teach you.

My years of watching skiers put their ski boots on has been instructive. So many suffer needlessly, depriving themselves of comfort and skier ecstasy. In this chapter, a little scientific knowledge goes a long way.

But, if you're feeling patronized by talking about how to put your boots on, fine. Skip this section and go to the next one. But, don't send me a nastygram if those new ski boots I just helped you buy result in agony the first day you try to ski in them.

The fact is, many skiers and even some newbie ski shop salespeople don't know how to put ski boots on. Oh sure, they get the right boots on the right feet. Almost everyone can do that. (Yes, there was a person who came to my ski lesson with their boots on the wrong feet. I asked him if his boots were comfortable. He replied cheerily, "Yes!" No harm, no foul.)

The problem is that many people suffer with ski boot pain as a result of putting their boots on wrong.

*To Help Assure Ski Holiday Bliss, Understand the Science of Ski Boot Donning*

The proper method of putting ski boots on is based on two scientific facts. You learned these facts in high school so you could pass two or three stupid quizzes. Then you quickly forgot them, squeezing them out of your mind so you could make more room for thoughts about sports and sex. That's because school teaches you a bunch of useless drivel that you never use in the real world.

Well, life comes full circle here, my friend. Your ability to guess the right answers below will have a direct impact on whether you experience pleasure or pain in your ski boots…

Here is our quiz:

Question 1: What's your body mostly composed of?

a) 60% water?

b) 52% whatever you ate in the last year?

Question 2: What will most slowly draw heat from your skin?

a) 60-degree Fahrenheit water?

b) 60-degree plastic?

c) 60-degree air?

Question 1 should be a "gimmee". We'll come back to that one.

Let's start with question two. What will most slowly draw heat from your skin, 60-degree water, plastic or air? This question might remind you of, "Which weighs more, a pound of iron or a pound of feathers?" But, this is different.

The correct answer is "c". 60-degree air will take longer to cool your skin than 60-degree water or 60-degree plastic in a ski boot. That's because air is a poor conductor of heat. Air insulates. In fact, the insulation in the walls of your home works by trapping pockets of air. These pockets act as barriers between comfortable interior temperatures and the bone chilling cold outside.

So, you ask, what does this have to do with putting ski boots on? Most recreational skiers make the mistake of associating more socks with more comfort and warmth inside a ski boot. More socks equate to more padding, comfort and warmth, right?

Wrong.

That's why most ski shops encourage skiers to wear one thin sock for skiing. Several years ago, when my relatively new ski boots refused to succumb to my best efforts to stretch, soften and mold to my feet, a good friend suggested that I take my socks off.

She offered a pair of her knee-high panty hose as replacements. They provided just enough barrier for my clammy feet to slide into my boots.

I was skeptical. I thought my toes would freeze and my shins would ache. But they didn't. In fact, I've been skiing ever since, even on sub-zero days, with nothing more than panty hose on my feet. My feet have stayed as warm and comfortable as anyone else's on the hill.

So, how is this possible?

By removing my socks, I created just a little more room for an air pocket to form in the toe boxes of my boots. My toes make contact only with the foot bed of the boot, not the fronts or tops, unless I'm curling my toes upward. Because my boot shells are clear plastic, I can actually see that I've created about a $1/8^{th}$ to ¼ inch barrier of warm air between my inner boot and the outer shell. This is what's insulating my toes from the cold!

Replacing my socks with panty hose has also improved my ability to feel surfaces inside the boot as I move against the ski, and the ski interacts with the snow. Before, when I wore socks, it would take about half a day before my socks "sealed" the bond between my feet and boots.

Some skiers describe this as "dialing in their boots" and if it happens, it's usually around midday. My boots are the high performance kind and very close fitting, so I was never in danger of my feet bouncing around inside an overly large shell. The panty hose work just right.

So, if you're unable to get comfortable due to boot pain or cold toes, examine your sock situation. You should never be wearing cotton socks or thick hiking socks. Either a thin wool sock...or panty hose, or nothing. I know it's counterintuitive. Just try it.

I alluded a minute ago to your ability to feel the inside of your ski boot, which is critical to skiing. You need to sense where you're standing against your skis, whether on the balls of your feet or the heels, whether you're pressing against the inside edge of the ski or the outside.

To do that, many skiers over-tighten their boots in the morning, which brings me to the answer to the first question.

So, is your body made mostly of water or what you've eaten in the last year? Assuming, you're not simply a collection of what you've dropped into your mouth, like a sock puppet, the correct answer is, "water". Your body is 60% watery mush, held together by leathery straps, pulleys and a network of calamari-like muscles.

So, how do you use this valuable science lesson to put your boots on properly? It starts by understanding that you're encasing your water balloon feet in adjustable casts.

If you clamp down your buckles in the morning at the same settings you used at the end of your last ski day, you're going to be in pain. During the course of a ski day, ski boots slowly squeeze bodily fluids out of your feet toward your heart. If you over-tighten your buckles, particularly around your shins, you'll cut off the flow of fluids into and out of your ski boots. That'll make even a well-fit boot hurt.

There are a few things to look out for when you're putting ski boots on. Hold the boot by the top of the tongue and back cuff as you slip your foot inside. Slide your heel gently to the back of the boot and begin cinching the buckles from the toes up. This is where things can go awry first thing in the morning.

I've seen many skiers for whom buckle cinching becomes a contest of who can tighten the tightest and snap their buckles the loudest. Remember, you need only close the boot around your foot comfortably, not clamp down with vise-like pressure.

After you've closed all the buckles, stand up and bend your knees and ankles. Your heels should slide back a little more into the heel pocket. You should be able to wiggle your toes. If you gently stand on the balls of your feet, the boot should comfortably hold your heels down. If any buckles feel uncomfortably loose, adjust as needed.

Start your ski day with your ski boots just snug enough to safely get to the top of the mountain. Then as you ski, adjust or tighten in small increments, as needed.

If you can't feel your soles against your boot bottoms without overtightening your buckles, you may be a candidate for custom molded foot beds. These fill in the gaps between your foot and your boot bottom. Footbeds can improve your skiing and your circulation. Most ski shops can make footbeds for you. Your feet will thank you.

# 8

# PERFECTLY PERFORMING SKIWEAR
# ON THE CHEAP

The principle of warm-air bubble wrap insulation applies with clothing as it did with ski boots. (See how to put on ski boots in the previous chapter). Today's ski clothing is lighter and has more warm air trapping properties than ski outfits of old. At least, that's the kind of ski wear you'll probably want to wear when you want to stay warm and cozy.

For those who are looking to abandon the mountain for action in the base lodge, there are chilly alternatives just for you. Find form-fitting ski jackets and pants that don't leave any room for thermal underwear underneath. If you don't mind a little more hypothermia, you can even go commando or, if you're more conservative, wear a thong. Guys, too. See you in the taverna!

But, if you're looking for skiwear that will keep you warm, dry and adaptable to changing weather conditions, read on. Let's start from the layer closest to your skin.

Note the word, "layers". Layers give you options. You can adapt comfortably when your chilly 10 °F morning warms to a balmy 40 degree afternoon. On most ski days, you'll be exposed to temperatures of 32 °F or lower and possibly some wind for several hours. Your base layer, the layer on your skin, should be of a material that insulates you from the cold and wicks sweat off your body.

Avoid wearing cotton as your base layer. Cotton is what bar mops are made out of. Bar mops soak up and retain fluids. Wet cotton won't keep you warm. Polyester fleece-lined underwear is an excellent base layer and an inexpensive, but important addition to your winter wear.

The second layer, over your base layer, should provide additional loft for trapping warm air. Polyester fleece jackets work great. Ideally this layer and your outer most layer should zip from neck to waist, so you can regulate air flow around your body. This enables you to adapt quickly as weather conditions change.

There are lots of choices for outer layers, often called shells. That's because they protect you from wind, rain…and rocks. (Just seeing if you're paying attention.) Shells are typically made of nylon and are lighter than coats.

If you're trying skiing or snowboarding for the first time, follow my advice on base and insulating layers. You can use inexpensive polyester fleece sweatshirts and a nylon jacket and nylon pants as your starter outfit. Later on, when you're hooked on skiing or snowboarding, you can invest in a jacket and pants that repel water and provide greater wind protection. These will be more costly but worth it.

There are several brand names of water- and wind-proof materials that are sewn into snow sportwear. Basically, they all work similarly. These ski apparel have large tags on them promoting their wind- and water-proof properties and justifying prices that give all of us sticker shock. But, if you're an avid skier or boarder, investing a few hundred in skiwear that will keep you comfortable for the next decade serves as mental lubricant for enduring such wallet penetration.

Find a shell with a hood. Your hood is a prized countermeasure against a sub-zero, 30 mile an hour wind pounding you on an eight-minute lift ride into the death zone. No, hoods won't invite the same bullying you endured in the eighth grade. Hoods are cool and expected at a ski resort.

I prefer shells over coats. A shell is very lightly lined or has no lining at all. I'm not looking for insulation from my shell. I have insulating sweaters for that. I'm looking for protection from wind and rain and the ability to zip up or down, depending on whether I'm getting too warm or too cold.

Ski coats are thicker. They often use goose down or other insulating materials to provide warmth. The problems with coats (for me, your humble Sherpa guide) are twofold:

They obviate (our three-dollar word in this section. Look it up you lazy lout,) the need for that lofty, fleecy mid layer. So, with just a thin base layer underneath, you've got this thick, warm coat encasing your skin, which makes it harder to circulate air around your sweaty body when you want to. The second problem is even if you unzip your coat, your arms and back are still encased in this bedding. I gave up on ski coats long ago. It's a matter of personal taste.

Okay, so you've got your base layer, insulating layers and shell. That works on upper and lower body. Change, add or delete layers as weather conditions dictate.

For most ski days, you'll want to wear a ski hat that covers your ears or a ski helmet, and goggles. Also, carry a neck gaiter to cover your neck and face when it gets very cold, snowy or windy.

Beginners, take heed! A ski hat, neck gaiter and goggles are small, inexpensive items that you can put on to quickly warm up or remove to cool off. You'll love them. Wear them or stash them in your pockets whenever you're on the piste.

# 9

# CHOOSING THE RIGHT SKIS:
# 10 THINGS TO LOOK FOR

After getting the right ski boots (and learning how to put them on without risking gangrene) and finding clothing that will keep you dry and comfortable as weather conditions change, skis are your third priority.

"*Third* priority?", you ask? Seems counterintuitive, I know.

Here's the deal. If your boots are comfortable and you're warm and dry, then you'll be 90% on your way to becoming a happy skier or snowboarder for life. The remaining 10% is about finding skis, which is easy to do, and a good professional ski instructor to teach you.

So, what distinguishes the right pair of skis for you?

Your ski choices are determined by your skiing ability, how often you ski, the snow conditions where you live, how frequently you'll fly to ski destinations and how committed you are to a certain kind of ski performance. OK, this sounds like calculus. It's not. Let's break this down.

So, do you ski four or fewer days per year? Skis have a useful life of about 120 ski days. So, skiing four days per year, it'll take you 30 years to get your money's worth out of any skis you buy. Your fellow ski lift riders will admire your vintage boards around the ten-year mark. At the twenty-year mark, they'll just assume you're old, homeless and crazy.

You don't want the same pair of skis for twenty years. Ski technology evolves and that's part of the allure of the sport.

By renting skis four days a year, you'll spend only about $120 US each season on skis. You'll always have access to more-or-less current ski technology at ski rental shops. You won't have to pay to have someone tune your skis. You'll avoid paying baggage fees at airports to transport your skis if you fly. Baggage fees add up quickly, averaging $35 *each way* on my last ski trip involving flights.

Renting skis is perfect for beginners and makes life easier for more advanced skiers as well. You'll have less to carry to and from your car. There won't be any ski tips jammed into the ribs of whoever is sitting in the passenger's seat.

If you're a better skier and want to rent demos (short for "demonstration skis") at rental shops, you'll need to pay a little more, maybe $180 US per year if your ski four days. Still not a bad deal considering that buying a performance ski and binding package will set you back $500 to $1200 U.S.

By demo-ing different kinds of skis, you'll also become far more able to discover your ski preferences. Some skis make large turns. Some make short turns. Some skis work best on ice and perform terribly in powder. Some skis are stable at high speeds and harder to turn at slower speeds.

It's all a matter of how the skis *feel* when you're skiing the way you like to ski. Are they fighting you on the hill? Or, do they give you a ride that culminates in whooping, fist bumping skier escstasy?

If you're skiing more than ten days a year, you should consider buying skis. This is particularly true if you're renting demos and have a good idea of what kind of ski you want. To pay $800 US over a couple of ski seasons to continue renting demo skis is a bit over the top. Buy skis for that much and you can enjoy them for the next five to ten years.

If you're skiing between five and ten days a year, you could go either way, rent or buy. Many skiers fall into this "nether-category". If you're renting or demo-ing skis, then buying will become more attractive when certain planets align…or when you know what kind of ski you want and find it at the right price.

Demo-ing and skiing on different kinds of skis is the best way of finding a ski that suits you perfectly. When you find a ski you like, take a photo of it. Then search for that ski in ski shops and online. This is the best way I know to find the ski you want and buy them.

So, what ski should you be looking for?

*Beginner or Wedge Turner*

If you're skiing at slow speeds or your skis are sweeping snow to the sides like a snow plow, then rental shop skis will work perfectly. If you're skiing frequently and considering buying skis, then something in the sub-$500 US category is suitable. You don't need expensive, stiff, high performance skis.

Find a softer flexing, entry level ski. When you stand beginner skis on end they should come up to about chest height. They're shorter so you can turn them easily and with less concern about crossing your tips.

Don't bother demo-ing high performance skis. That can come later when you become more skilled at cutting the snow surface with your edges rather than sweeping the snow with the bottoms of your skis.

### Intermediate or if You Ski "Parallel" Sometimes

Rental shop skis will work well for you, too. If you're skiing at the pace of most other skiers on the blue runs or passing other skiers, you could start demo-ing high performance skis. This will give you a sense of the different kinds of skis out there.

As an intermediate, you'll also probably be looking for a ski that's more stable at higher speeds than the skis you used as a beginner. That'll usually mean a longer ski, one that reaches from the floor to about your chin. This will expand your skiing platform like the wheelbase of a car.

### Advanced – Expert Skier

If you're skiing parallel all the time and hitting the black diamonds regularly, you're ready to move beyond rental shop skis. You should be on a high performance "all-mountain" ski or a recreational racing ski.

All-mountain skis come in two flavors. The first is a front side carver. This will be the board of choice for skiers who are usually skiing on packed powder or hard, icy snow. The second kind of all-mountain ski is more suitable for powder skiers. These skis are much easier to turn through several inches...or even a few feet...of fresh powder.

All-mountain powder skis are wider and softer flexing than front-side carving skis. The tips of powder skis are wide and soft so they bend upward when moving through powder. This helps the ski float on top of deep, fresh snow and makes it easier to make turns in the "steep and deep".

Stiffer, narrower all-mountain skis are for hard snow. They have less flex in tips and tend to dive in powder but can provide more assured edge-hold on groomed trails and icy snow.

As you travel closer to the resorts themselves, you'll encounter the shamans who know the ways of the local snow gods. Just ask them, and they will channel you to the right mountains, slopes, lifts, lodging, skis and restaurants (with the exception of off-trail ski runs in the woods that constitute their private stash.)

If you have several hours to spare and want to watch skiers give reviews of different skis online, then you could actually learn more about the performance characteristics of each ski. If you have no personal experience with different skis, then recommendations from several experienced skiers who've skied on them can be helpful.

Above all, don't stress too much about ski choices. Get out on the slopes and have a good time with whatever boards you own or rent.

Choosing skis can be challenging. You can't try them on in the shop like you do ski boots or clothing. You can't tell which ski fits your weight, strength or skiing style by looking at it. That's why demo-ing different skis is so helpful. Short of demo-ing, some skiers buy skis based on the graphics glued to their tops. That's not the side they ski on, but what they heck, they look good.

That's fine if you're a beginner and haven't developed the sensitivity to distinguish between different skis' performances. But, if you've progressed to the point where you've experienced a run that exhilarated you beyond the ability to utter consonants, by the sensations of natural forces upon your being and the kinesthetic joy of balancing against them, then you can probably discern between different skis' performance characteristics.

Most customers who ask ski shop salespeople for advice about what ski to buy are beginning or intermediate skiers. In many cases, these skiers haven't yet developed the sensitivity to distinguish how different skis turn. So, almost any mid-priced "all around" ski will do. That's not a bad thing.

Go forth to the mountains with whatever boards you happen to have and play.

*Park Skier*

Here's where the industry creates a lot of excitement targeting aspiring daredevils looking to show off their best tricks skiing over jumps, buses and whatever else park crews have embedded in the snow.

Everything I described so far in this chapter about matching skis with your ability and performance still applies. You can continue to home in on the best skis for you by answering one simple question: How much of your ski day will you spend in parks grinding over rails and doing jumps versus free skiing the entire mountain?

If you're spending most of your day in the park, then you'll be doing less mountain skiing and more acrobatic moves at moderate speeds. You'll need skis that are maneuverable—skis that are shorter, narrower and, if you're going to be skiing backwards, have the tails upturned like the tips. You'll also need to accept that your skis' edges will be dull from all that grinding.

If, on the other hand, you're going to be skiing all over the mountain, jumping off cornices and blasting through whatever snow conditions come your way, you're going to want a ski that's more stable at higher speeds and more versatile in different snow conditions. That's generally going to mean a ski that is longer, wider and with sharper edges than if you only skied in the park.

Of course, there are no absolutes with skis. With enough skill, you can get any kind of ski to do roughly anything you want. And, like I said a minute ago, the point is to have fun whatever you're skiing on.

Just keep in mind that different kinds of skis have performance strengths. If your current skis aren't stable enough at higher speeds, your next pair should be longer and stiffer. If they don't float in powder, your next pair should be more flexible and wider. If you want more maneuverability, go shorter and less stiff. You could even consider ski blades, which are just long enough to mount bindings on them.

Of course, you can solve all your ski choice conundrums by collecting a quiver of multiple pairs of skis, each designed to perform in different snow conditions.

If you're still living on your parents' dime, you'll need to make the case to your folks that owning two or three pairs of skis is absolutely essential to your successful journey into adulthood.

If you've already left your parents' nest, earn money and want to invest in several pairs of skis, congratulations! You've got lots of skis to choose from and too much money for your own good. Please unburden yourself of some of that financial responsibility by sending a check to Dan, last name spelled C-O-D-Y.

Thanks.

*Now, if You Really Want to Get into the Nitty-Gritties about Skis…*

This section is for my diehard skier friends around the world who love to talk about the engineering and performance characteristics of various ski designs. And, as long as we're jumping into the deep end here, let's throw in the biomechanics and physics of skiing, too.

It's all one big happy discussion among ski instructors around the world fueled mostly by nachos and beer. And, as you'll soon see, everyone eventually comes to similar conclusions about how to find the right skis for you—demo them. But, I digress.

Skis are designed to turn. That's how most of us control our speed and direction on ski hills. Occasionally, you'll encounter a small minority who ski straight down the hill. They rely on butt-brakes to stop, which is discouraged by ski instructors and health care professionals.

One of a ski's characteristics that determines whether it's better at making *skidded* turns or *carved* turns is its *flex pattern*. If you put two skis together bottom to bottom, the tips and tails touch and the middles don't. That gap in the middle is caused by the skis' *camber*.

Camber helps distribute your weight over the tips and tails when you stand on the middle of the ski. How much weight that is required to bend the middle of a ski below its tip or tail is called *longitudinal flex*. Skis that are longitudinally stiffer push the tips and tails down more into the snow.

Most skis are stiffer in the tails than the tip. We shift our weight *slightly* to the tail to stop a turn and *slightly* forward to the tips to start a turn. So, a ski's tail is usually stiffer because it has to serve as strong platform at the end of a turn, where the centrifugal force generated by the skier's turn and gravity align.

Ski tips are softer flexing to absorb bumps and conform more easily to the shape of the new turn. That's where we're just beginning to pivot, tilt and shift our weight on to the new turning ski. (If the idea of standing mostly on the *turning ski* or *downhill ski* is completely foreign to you, now is an excellent time to take a ski lesson…and skip to the concluding paragraph of this section!)

*Rockers*—not musicians, but skis built with *reverse camber* near the tips—actually pre-conform to the arcs of early stage turns. That makes initiating turns with them easier.

If that's not confusing enough, there's also *torsional stiffness*. That's how much the ski twists along its longitudinal axis when it's tilted on edge. More twisting means the tips and tails will provide less edge hold. High performance skis twist less. They tend to be torsionally stiffer than beginner skis.

Each pair of skis bends in predictable ways that will feel better or worse depending on your weight and ability. Lighter and less technically adept skiers are usually happier on shorter, softer flexing skis. Heavier and more skilled skiers generally favor a stiffer ski, especially on hard pack or icy snow.

The *sidecut* also influences how skis turn. Because skis are narrower in the middle than in the tips and tails, they scribe an arc when gliding with them tilted on the snow. The more radical the sidecut, the more quickly the ski will scribe a short radius turn. Less sidecut is better for longer turns and stability at higher speeds.

So, there you have it. Now, you can walk into any ski shop where salespeople will be astonished with your deep knowledge of ski design.

Or, rather than attempting to calculate which ski will work best for you, you can rent demos and try skiing on different skis. If you've already got a sense for how skis of different shapes and flex patterns feel, you could also Google "online ski reviews". As I mentioned earlier, these reviews by skiers can be informative and entertaining.

*Money-Saving Ski Buying Tips*

If you've demoed skis and know what you want, you can search at ski shops and online for an unused pair from a recent ski season. Some ski shops will cut you a deal to sell their previous season's unsold equipment.

Alternatively, you can go to local ski swaps. These are usually held in fall and early spring. There, you'll meet skiers who are selling their used equipment, usually at bargain basement prices. When you buy skis second-hand, be sure to have them checked by a certified ski technician. That way, you'll know you got a great deal on skis and bindings that will perform well and are safe to use.

Also, check out deals on new equipment at your local ski shop. Many shops create economical packages that include skis, bindings and other ski equipment. You can talk to knowledgeable salespeople who will help you find the perfect setup.

# 10

# TIRES. YEAH, TIRES

I know. Tires don't get you stoked, but bear with me. I'm not talking about what tires you drive into ski country. We all know snow tires will work better than city driving slicks. Those old summer tires that melted to a flat, treadless moonscape during last summer's vacation in Death Valley won't work as well. (You *do* know this, right?)

I'm not even going to talk about the vehicle you should be driving into ski country. You should already know this, too. Front wheel drive is good. Four-wheel drive, better. Four-wheel drive with high clearance, best. That high bottom helps you hurdle snowy berms and places where you thought you turned into a driveway, but it turned out to be an 8-inch curb. I speak from experience.

So, what do I mean when I say, "Tires"? I mean your tires contact with the snow. You don't need a $90,000 Humvee to drive in snow. You need to manage what your tires are doing on the road.

Most of the accidents, ditchings and near misses I've seen on mountain roads have been the result of driver error. Sure, it would help if you had a Jeep. But, when driving over a snowy mountain pass, I'd rather follow a guy driving a KIA Optima who's savvy about winter driving than a clueless sunbird in a Humvee any day. That's because whatever mistakes the guy in front of me makes, I have to live with.

If he stops, I have to stop. And, of course, it will be driving uphill. So, getting moving again is going to require deft feathering of torque to my drive wheels so as not to spin them. This will be accompanied by my loud cursing with my car windows closed.

So, let's cover what your tires should be doing when you're driving icy roads leading to many ski resorts.

A) They should not be skidding…ever, in any direction.

That's it. Just A.

If this sounds deceptively simple, it's not. See, tires want to skid in all directions; not just your tires, but everyone else's around you.

So, you have to not only watch out for, but also anticipate, what your vehicle and their vehicles are going to do once they lose traction. In this respect, driving in winter conditions is a lot like hockey. Unlike hockey, though, you have to drive to where the pucks, *won't* be.

It takes ten times longer to stop a car on ice than on a dry road. That's if you're on a level roadway. If you're going downhill on ice, you may never stop, no matter how long or skillfully you apply your brakes.

One evening while leaving Heavenly ski resort, I developed a new appreciation of what it would be like to slide down a luge track in my car. It had snowed for a couple of days before. Temperatures that morning had been in the low 40s. The sun had beaten down on nearby roads causing sheets of slush to melt. By late afternoon clouds came in and the temperature dropped about 25 degrees. I left the base lodge after quaffing a beer with my fellow instructors.

It was dark, about six pm by the time I left to drive down one of the neighborhood access roads into town. This was off the beaten path, a side route only the locals knew about. It wasn't trafficked enough to clear the road of snow or ice.

I exited the parking lot and felt the terrain roll off down the hill ahead. In the distance, about 500 feet in front of me, I could make out what appeared to be hazard lights and brake lights from multiple cars strewn across the road.

I was going about 25 mph when I hit my brakes. Nothing. Then, I gently feathered and tapped my brakes lightly to try to get some purchase on the road surface. That gave me just enough grip to steer with some effect but I wasn't slowing down. I was the bowling ball about to hit the pins, resulting in tens of thousands of dollars in damage and the possibility of hurting people. This is not where a destitute ski instructor should be.

My only hope of slowing down was to rub the right side of my car against the snow berm that had piled up along the street in the days before. The nose of my car would be the first to touch the berm. I was worried about the damage I'd do to my car. I figured I'd probably lose the right front headlight and fender, but that was all. But I also knew that, if the nose caught too quickly, I could spin around and wind up careening down the hill backwards into the tangle of cars and people below.

This is one of those moments where you age. You're reminded of all the admonishments your parents gave you to be careful and realize, this is the moment they were trying to prepare you for. You know that if you get out of this alive and reasonably intact, you're probably going to be driving a little bit more like the old man. Yeah, an old man wearing a brimmed hat who's always driving in front of you on a one lane road at 10 miles per hour below the speed limit.

The snow and ice began tearing up the side of my car as I maneuvered just enough to rub the berm. I felt the car begin to slow and I expected that the back end would come around any moment, but it didn't. My car finally stopped moving within about 150 feet of the start of my intentional ditching. I expected to be hit from the rear any second by another hapless victim of the ice. My rear view mirror was clear.

After a few seconds of collecting myself, I opened the door and promptly slipped and fell on my butt. After steading myself on all fours, looking like a newly birthed fawn, I began skitching down the hill to see if I could help untangle the mess of cars below. I clearly wasn't going back up the hill. My only path home was down!

In this instance and others where Mother Nature's sees fit to turn a road into a dangerous luge track, you've got to respect the ice. Remember you may only have 10% of the stopping power you would on dry roads. So, here's the cardinal rule for driving on snow packed roads:

Avoid skidding, slipping, sliding. At the risk of sounding like your grade school teacher who demanded that you recite your ABC's ad infinitum, let me repeat that avoid skidding sounds simpler than it is. It requires *anticipation*.

As I've demonstrated, going down an icy road is one of the most dangerous driving challenges. Even if you carefully control your speed, you can still find yourself in a dangerous situation where you can't stop in time.

Anticipate what you would do if the road were blocked in front of you. Regulate your speed accordingly. If you can't stop within the distance that you can see ahead of you, *you're going too fast.*

Local residents around ski resorts adapt to ice-road driving by cutting their speed, sometimes by half of the posted speed limit. In contrast, it's the impatient, iPhone-distracted, life at click-speed city slickers (yes, like *you*) who drive as if a salted road absolves them of taking precautions.

If you don't want to stand out as a weekender who hasn't a clue, then drive like a local. Sure, your out of state license plate gives you away. That's OK. The point is not to *act* as if you're clueless.

As I said, driving up and down hilly, icy roads requires anticipation. This is really where you separate the men from the boys, and the women from the girls. It's also where you separate clueless drivers from their passengers who have to get out and push their rides out of snow berms.

I have passed four-wheel drives who could not make it up the same hill I was driving in my Honda Accord. Why? Because they stopped on their way up the hill. They lost momentum from the run up to the hill. What little purchase their tires had on the icy surface is all for naught for these little birdies. They'll either need to put their chains on if they have chains, back down the hill or wait until road conditions change.

By the way, having lived at Lake Tahoe, I've had ample occasions to put chains on. I can tell you this. Putting chains on your tires is a lot like eating raw kale. It's a good thing to do, but it's unpleasant. Doubly unpleasant if you have to put chains on the rear drive wheels.

You can't see where the chain ends connect on the side of the tire facing the underside of the car. So, you'll need to crawl around your cold, wet, salty, muddy tire in your $600 US ski outfit while your exposed fingers trying to get the ends of the chain to link up.

Depending on the temperature, that cold steel chain will draw all the heat out of your fingers within ten to 30 seconds, rendering your hands completely numb. Now, not only can you not see the ends of the chain, you can't feel them either. I call this the "Hellen Keller" syndrome. If you get through the chain up process without verbalizing multiple expletives, you're a better person than me.

Of course, there will be times when highway conditions (and the state troopers) will require that you have chains on. If you're planning to drive mountain passes or places with frequent, deep snows, it's a good idea to pack chains in your trunk. But, we want to avoid having to put chains on (which will result in your having to take them off again) if possible.

So, here's how to drive up an icy, long hill:

The key is to maintain a consistent speed. Don't stop until you get over the top, to level roadway again. If you can see that traffic is moving at a consistent speed right over the top, no worries. But, if traffic is stop and go and cars are spinning their wheels to get moving again up the hill, wait until the route to the top is clear. Wait until you can get some momentum in the flats and carry it up the hill.

This is going to require some gumption. The locals and experienced winter driving Ninjas behind you will appreciate your methods. But, you can imagine what the non-Ninja, city slicker, latte quaffing weekenders are screaming at their windshields, as they wait behind what looks like a widening gulf of open road in front of you. If they're insistent, wave them passed you. You, my friend, are going to the top of this slush pile.

We haven't yet talked about sideways skidding. Sure, if you take turns too fast, you're going to slide. Remember, a good guess for the right road speed on snowy roads is about half the posted speed limit. Adjust from there going up and down hills and when making turns.

The fact is that most sideways skids that I've seen aren't the result of left or right turns. They're the result of lane changes. Typically, snow piles up between traffic lanes as tires push snow to the sides. Often, snow collects in the center of the lane, directly underneath your car and between lanes. These are the culprits that cause so many spin outs.

When changing lanes, the tires on one side of your car can get bogged down in these snow piles while the tires on the other side of car wisp along unencumbered. When that happens, you're going into a flat spin, Maverick. And, you're Top Gun ski vacation days could come to a spectacular close with your back end plowing the median. Watch your tires, Mav!

# 11

# HOW TO CARRY YOUR SKIS WITHOUT LOOKING LIKE YOU'RE HOLDING A BROKEN HELICOPTER

We're talking about moving you, your skis, boots, clothing, and everything else you need for skiing from your home, to your car to the ski resort and back. Spoiler alert. We're going to talk about Dan Cody's patent pending system for transporting your gear. If you already have a system that works well, then this section is optional, unless you answer yes to either of these two questions:

Do you look like you're carrying parts of a helicopter, skis, poles, gloves askew, laundry basket style as you approach the base lodge?

Or, do you find that you or someone else in your group manages to forget their hat or gloves and not realize that they've forgotten them until they reach the ski lift?

As you've already surmised, my intelligent friend, this section is about assuring that you'll have with you all the skiing accoutrements you'll need for a fun day on the slopes.

I've seen portage problems play out in a couple of ways…

Forgotten hats and gloves are one. For some reason, these are the forgotten items of choice among children. In fact, in the U.S., children under seventeen years old can't be trusted to pack properly for ski vacations. This is because children in the U.S. don't have as much experience skiing as children in countries where skiing is a national sport.

In Norway, for example, children as young as six are sent alone into the sub-zero night on wooden skis to fetch Chinese takeout from nearby villages. "And, dunt let da dimsum get kuld agaiyn, Torrill!" You think these kids forget their hats and gloves?

Kids in the United States think that if they can walk five minutes through the snow to the bus stop wearing nothing but a hoodie they've enough cold weather know-how to survive on Mount Everest's death zone. So, they don't need hats or gloves at ski resorts. So what if it's 20 degrees, the wind is howling and they're going to be outside for the next six hours?

"I'll be too waaaaarm! That hat looks stupid. I won't need it."

In the U.S., some kids will purposely *avoid* bringing essential warm weather gear even though they know they'll need it.

I have a theory about this.

The theory is that teens, particularly in the U.S., are distracted from wearing proper ski wear by hormonal changes they're experiencing. I know I'm way ahead of the scientific community on this. Kids look down their own shorts and think, wow, I can have children soon. That must also mean that I'll also be able to drive, earn money and do whatever I want, including defy extreme cold.

With teenage boys, particularly, you've got the hormonal urge to prove how macho they are. Can they go shirtless when it's 20 degrees out? Of course they can, especially if their hormonally-impaired teenage buddies are doing it.

Why bother with hats, gloves…or *coats*…for that matter!

You've got to remember that teenagers have to show up at the same place every day where dozens, possibly hundreds, of other hormonally whacked out peers show up. And unlike you and I, teenagers can't just quit their jobs and move on if they don't fit in. So, there's a real incentive to avoid becoming a target of ridicule.

Better for them to leave that stupid looking hat at home. That way your child won't draw the ire of little fashion police who will group text his or her demise by lunch period. For kids, it's OK to freeze, as long as they don't show weakness.

You and I also know that within forty-five minutes of stepping outside into the cold ski resort air without their hats, these very same teenagers will whine at you. It won't matter that hours before you told them to bring their hats. You won't feel better for reminding them of that now either.

You'll be at the top of the mountain with a teen who's warning you that they'll soon be hypothermic and frost bitten.

They'll say it just loudly enough for the adults around you to hear.

Teens will use this occasion to their advantage. They will publicly suggest that you don't you love them anymore because you should know how stupid a teenager is and you should have secretly stashed a ski hat in your parka for them to wear. You thought your job stopped at parent. Not on ski trips. You are also porter, responsible for lugging your progeny's ski gear.

For those of you who ignore my advice about waiting to start your children skiing until they can pay for and carry their own skis, which for some will be their mid-thirties, the upshot is this…

NEVER! EVER! EVER! count on your child to bring all the warm weather gear they'll need to a ski resort. They will go out of their way *not* to bring something and it will be your fault. They will also remind you that it's your responsibility to get them what they need.

This isn't to say that experienced adult skiers don't forget items, too. Take insulating layers (which we talked about in the clothing chapter.) What do you do if you've forgotten that much needed fleece jacket to keep you warm? Blow $100 US on a new fleece sweater in the resort shop or go back to the hotel to retrieve it.

Meanwhile, your friends are still on the mountain. If they're waiting for you, they'll be gracious, but impatient. That's because of skiing's cost factor.

When you include transportation, lodging, lift tickets and equipment, the actual on-slope time can cost as much as a dollar a minute. If your friends are not waiting for you, finding them will take you another hour after you've found your fleece jacket. A forgotten and replaced pair of mittens can cost you 90 minutes, about $90, before you're back with your friends doing what you came to the ski resort to do, ski and have fun!

So, we're going to talk about a system that assures you'll have what you need and can carry it easily to and from the ski lodge to your car.

But first, an object lesson in why this system could save your ski day. It only takes the briefest distraction to put you in a foul mood, one where skier ecstasy will be nearly impossible, at least for a day.

I was demoing skis on a weeklong trip at Lake Tahoe. A group of us were skiing different resorts each day. On the way to Squaw Valley one morning, we stopped at a ski shop to rent powder skis. I brought one of my ski boots into the shop so the ski tech could adjust the binding to my boot.

Well, you already know this ends badly.

Driving the access road to Squaw Valley is enough to get your heart pounding. You pass the Olympic rings at the entrance to the valley. The steep white peaks rise up on either side supported by massive stone buttresses. Their size grows until you reach the base lodge. The terrain is big, steep, varied and fun.

So, imagine my delight upon parking and opening the back of the SUV to retrieve my ski boots. My morning at Squaw Valley flung away like a pumpkin tossed downfield by a pumpkin chunkin' catapult. I was one-bootless, and might as well have been completely bootless.

This is where a system for carrying my skier gear assumed a higher station on my pyramid of self-actualization.

Like the Joanie Mitchell song lyrics, "You don't know what you got till it's gone," the need to forego a sure thing is doubly painful when you've inflicted the damage on yourself.

Forgetting my boot at the ski shop forty minutes away meant that I had to ask an acquaintance if I could borrow his car (he graciously said yes), forego most of the morning's skiing to retrieve my boot at the ski shop and rendezvous with my friends later on the mountain. Not just a ski resort. A vast mountain complex of epic proportion, reputation and terrain, Squaw Valley. I had screwed up would could have been a perfect day of skiing at *Squaw Valley*.

The weather was perfect. The sun shone brightly in the blue morning sky as I turned the SUV onto the Squaw Valley access road, and drove back down to the highway. It was about 25 degrees. Snow crystals sparkled in the air as they fell off the trees. The sunlight danced on the lake. In front of me, lay my forgotten ski boot on a counter in a ski shop. Behind me were my friends, Squaw Valley. And, in my pocket was the $110 US I would hand over to Squaw Valley for a lift ticket. But, I would do that nearly 90 minutes later, 90 minutes *after* I should have. Then, I would start riding up the three levels of ski lifts to look for my friends. I'd already lost half a day of skiing nirvana and put myself in a very foul mood.

I share my humiliation and pain with you to illustrate the importance of knowing how to transport your ski gear in such a way that it all gets to where you need it, when you need it.

*How to Carry Your Stuff Across the Ski Resort Parking Lot*

Any ski equipment you don't rent at the resort has to be carried. Unless you're Bon Jovi and have roadies who'll move your stuff for you, the pack mule will be you. This is a special opportunity to look and feel like you have your stuff together. You can glide across the parking lot with style and confidence, or you could look like your goal is to do your laundry in the base lodge.

By the way, you've noticed by now that I keep referring to carrying your gear between your car in the resort parking lot and the base lodge. If I put on my boots in the parking lot, I'd have to walk in them to the lift ticket window and then onto the snow.

But, I'm a big proponent of *not* walking ski boots. My boots were definitely not made for walking. I put them on in the base lodge.

There are two reasons for this. The first is comfort. If you've got any sensitive spots on your feet or shins, then you know a walk of some distance in ski boots is akin to saying, "Thank you sir, may I have another!"

The second reason is ski boots are plastic. The soles wear down easily on asphalt and cement. So, you could wear out a pair of boots from the bottoms, which I've done.

So, how does one get skis, poles, boots, insulating top and bottom layers, ski jacket and pants, socks, goggles, gloves, hat, gaiter, wallet, keys and phone from the car to the resort?

As we've talked about briefly here, one way is to put everything on except your skis at the car. I've used this method when I had only a few paces between my car and the lift ticket window. God bless small, well designed ski resorts.

But, when I've got to walk a quarter mile or more across a bomb-cratered parking lot or do a Lewis & Clark expedition through a phalanx of latte cafes, ski shops, clothing stores and bagelries that some sadistic ski resort planner has thoughtfully placed between my car and the lift ticket window, I carry my boots.

*Carrying Your Stuff Can Be Meditative. No really. It can.*

The walk in the morning to the resort greets you with crisp, cold air and the promise of fun. The walk back in the afternoon is time to glow and celebrate the day's adventure. You should enjoy this ritual, really. I do.

My ideal is toting half of what I need to carry on my back in a small day pack. My hat, gloves, goggles, top and bottom outer shells are in the pack. With everything rolled up, everything fits nicely.

I'll walk to the base lodge wearing my fleece top and bottom. I have lots of pockets in my fleeces. So, I can easily carry my keys, phone and wallet on me. That leaves the skis, poles and boots.

You can tote your skis and poles in a ski bag. That takes care of one hand. The other hand carries both boots by a tether. Simple.

Alternatively, you can sling both skis over one shoulder and grab your poles and the boot tether with the other. You'll look like you know what you're doing and you'll instantly command the admiration of your fellow skiers.

This is important. This is as much about feeling your mojo carrying your equipment through the parking lot as it is on the mountain.

# 12

# 6 SKIING TIPS THAT EVERY AMATEUR INSTRUCTOR SHARES

Before I impart my infinite wisdom on this topic, a few bona fides are required here. There's no reason to listen to me unless I can ante up first with some qualifications, right? So, here they are:

I taught skiing for five years. Three years were full time. I was a certified instructor. I devoted these five years to understanding physics, biomechanics, ski technique…and partying.

The ideas presented in this book are those that found homes in my brain during this period. Their finding homes was not easy. I confess that I was sometimes consuming one or two happy substances each day through this time. The fact that any ideas found their way through the fog in my head is testament to the profound value of those concepts, not my ability to learn anything while under herbal distractions…which, by the way, I don't recommend.

I also managed physical education skiing courses for schools and colleges between Monticello and Poughkeepsie, New York. A thousand kids each week would arrive at the resort at 5 pm, take lessons and try to find new places to make out in the base lodge. The majority also became skiers.

This stands in stark contrast to the dozens of ex-skiers I've met. Their spouses, lovers or friends attempted to teach them how to ski. And, the outcomes were in many cases, producing ex-skiers who'd never again strap on a pair of skis and, in some cases, ex-spouses or ex-friends.

It's usually a guy trying to teach his friend, often a woman, how to ski. She gets credit for being game enough to try skiing. Maybe she's ambitious enough to improve her skiing enough to keep up with her boyfriend or husband.

The guy loses points for teaching something he can't teach and expecting his girlfriend keep up with him. She shouldn't have to. Thankfully, most males skiers know this.

Hey, don't start writing me a nastygram about the equality of women! I've met several women on the slopes who've kicked my derriere. In some cases, they were competitive racers or freestyle skiers. These women were athletes who were training to win in their respective events. They worked cardio and strength in the off season. They were stronger, better skiers than I was. There are plenty of women who can out-ski most men. So, put your pen down. I'm not sexist.

It's just that most women have no ambition to ski better than a man. They're on vacation. And, when guys take it upon themselves to teach skiing to their girlfriends or wives, it plays out like a bad reality TV show.

And, you ask, from whence comes my super-human insight?

It comes from thousands of lift rides. During my rides up mountains, I trained my super-spy, parabolic long-range microphone downward toward to the slopes below to eavesdrop on skiers providing skiing tips to their hapless victims. I carefully noted their skills, the slopes they were skiing and their interaction with the aforementioned tip providers.

Before I tell you what I observed, let me share this: Of the hundreds of ski lessons I've taught, there were a portion, particularly later in my career, that catapulted my students forward toward skiers' nirvana. They wrote dozens of letters to my ski school director, testifying to my super-instructor awesomeness. (Of course, none of this appeared on my resume when I started looking for a "real" job, because prospective employers don't have much use for ex-ski instructors. Anyway...)

It took a lot of practice to learn how to teach skiing. These students benefited from a confluence (whoop, another three syllable word you'll have to look up, dude) of factors including:

- Their having the right equipment
- My understanding of their skiing goals
- Observing their skiing skills, athleticism and aggressiveness

- Identifying the thing that would improve their skiing and that they could begin to master in one hour.

- Taking them to the right slope, with the right snow conditions

- Communicating the thing they needed to know in a language they could absorb and use to ski better in minutes

Ok. I know ski instructors don't always command the same respect as clergy, public school teachers or even out-of-work musicians. But, most of us take ski teaching very seriously.

Being able to coach someone, to have them see improvement within an hour, is a real skill. So, compare the art of ski teaching I've just described to what I've observed of weekend warriors from my god-perch on the ski lift overhead:

"Face downhill!"

"Lean forward!"

"Bend your knees!"

"Keep your hands up!"

"Dig in your edges!"

"Turn!"

…To which the recipients of this advice follow this general path of responses:

"Okay."

"I am!"

"I can't! This isn't working, Jerry!"

"Fuck you, Jerry!"

And, just for the record, I have never heard, "Oh thanks, Jerry, this is working much better now."

So, my advice for teaching friends to ski is…

Don't.

Yes, you can bark the same six pieces of advice that every skier knows, but it will only serve to frustrate you and your victim. So, don't try to teach skiing. If you do, you'll probably provide the wrong advice and contribute to the 84% of first time skiers who never come back.

Leave it to the professionals. Even if they don't look like professionals because they barely shave and say, "stoked" too much. If your friend is beyond the beginner level, ask for a certified instructor. Certified instructors have passed exams that assure they are knowledgeable of ski technique and teaching methods and are competent skiers.

Swallow your pride. Lay out some cash for a lesson. If it does nothing else, it's a worthwhile investment in your relationship.

# 13

# HOW TO IMPROVE YOUR SKIING

"Tell me what I'm doing wrong."

"What do I need to work on?"

"I want to ski properly."

If you're an intermediate, advanced or expert skier, you've probably uttered these words at some point in your skiing career.

Most skiers are wired to work at things, to find the singular, best way of doing "it". It could be dicing onions, running a business or performing in a sport. We strive to be do it best or at least emulate those who do.

We're about reaching the ideal or appearing as if we have. Many of us don't spend much time soaking in the journey. But, that's where most of the rewards are.

Hey, I know I'm going a little Deepak Chopra on you here. Just bear with me.

For most people, skiing is not a job, nor should it ever become one. For me, five years of wearing a ski instructor's jacket became tiresome at times. Skiing "well" and "in control" and serving as a paragon of "good behavior" on the piste was the cost of my skiing for free. But, I was serving as an example of the "ideal". I had given up some parts of the journey that are important to me.

I skied far better after retiring from ski teaching. I was once again free to relax, experiment and *play with my skis*. I was on vacation again, able to ski sloppily if I wanted, make mistakes and fall without attracting the disapproving eyes of resort managers or guests.

I skied for fun, not money.

You ski for fun. Don't you? Fun can take different forms on skis. Maybe you ski to socialize. Or, perhaps, you enjoy the alpine air, mountain views, or because skiing feels good. Maybe you ski to show off. Skiing, after all, is a form of self-expression. Most of us ski for a combination of these reasons.

## It's About Expanding Your Repertoire

Whatever the reason for skiing, becoming a better skier is a result of a developing a wider repertoire of skills, not limiting yourself to a few pretty poses. Even as you make turns on a consistent, well-groomed pitch, the forces on your body change throughout each turn. So, too, should your body's responses to these forces change.

The best skiers exhibit continuous fluid movements on their skis, especially when linking turns. They are almost most *never*

THE SKIERS GIFT BOOK THAT'S SWEEPING THE GLOBE (SORT OF)

*not moving on their skis.* Yes, the double negative of that last sentence is intentional. Great skiers never stand motionless like statues on their skis.

They are constantly applying a subtle mix of forces to their skis. Their skis are also delivering an ever changing mix of forces back, to which skiers respond. When the forces applied by the skier produce predictable forces back from the skis, the skier looks balanced and controlled.

The best skiers are able to ski nearly any slope in the most challenging snow conditions. They make it *look* easy, but they are in fact playing with a series of linked emergencies!

Steep slopes with trees and snow that's been skied through for a couple of days, presents all kinds of challenges to skiers' wits and balance. All of these require adjustments…or a series of linked recoveries.

Will the next turn be in powder or on a skied off section of hard snow? Guessing wrong will force the skier to correct mid-turn. Are there obstacles below that the skier can't see but needs to avoid at the last minute? What happens if she misses a turn? How will she slow down?

Posers die in the trees. (That should be a bumper sticker.) Steeps, moguls, trees, variable snow conditions and other skiers force reactions that aren't always "pretty", but are athletic and effective.

If you're having fun exploring what your skis and body can do, you'll become a better skier, faster. What happens when you keep your skis flat on the snow? What if they're flat just at the beginning of a turn? How about on a gentle slope? What's it like to make turns on one foot?

What about that knoll on your favorite run? What's it like to go over it, to turn around it or to make two turns on top of it?

Can you turn as quickly when your hands are near your pant pockets versus holding them up?

Learning how to ski well is about developing a broad repertoire of skiing skills and movements. There will be a handful of "moves" that make up most of your skiing. But, learning how to adapt to terrain, snow conditions and your own fancy is really where the freedom of skiing comes from.

Do you want to slip leisurely through a few turns as you take in some mountain scenery? That's perfectly acceptable. Do you want to carve a few high-speed slices into the snow? That's fine, too.

### The Ski School Student's Challenge

"I want to ski with my skis more parallel or closer together," is a common desire expressed by skiers. It's a place where aesthetics is the priority and the mastery of a variety of skiing challenges temporarily takes a back seat.

This aesthetic desire is something we all have to varying degrees. Skiing is a form of self-expression. We all want to look graceful, scribing perfect arcs in snow, energetic, balanced, athletic and even *sexy*.

We all aspired early in our skiing careers to ski parallel. Getting both skis to do the same thing at the same time, even if both skis were doing the wrong thing, was a huge milestone for all of us. It was a weigh point at which we proved to the world (and skiers we thought were watching us) that we were no longer beginners. We were savvy, cool, advanced skiers.

The only places where having both skis jammed together counts for points is competitive mogul and aerial competitions…which most of us will never do.

So, it's up to our ski instructors to show us how to balance more consistently on our downhill ski. The other ski will drift closer quite naturally when that happens. Will this increase a skier's ability to ski the steeps or deep crud? It expands their skill set, so, yes it does.

Should most skiers actually ski with their skis jammed together? If you don't mind the clacking sound of your edges which you're dulling by the second, it's fine. But most skiers who do this will remain at the intermediate or advanced intermediate level because they're more concerned about looking a certain way than skiing well.

Ski aficionados (an elite club of which I'm a member and carry an official "ski aficionado" card) universally recognize World Cup racers as the best skiers on the planet.

OK, this is another topic about which many readers will write me nastygrams about why I'm wrong, naming skiers who are better than World Cup racers and so on. You want a piece of me, Sparky? Let's go.

Let's start with what World Cup racers actually do. Like their counterparts in freestyle skiing, X Games and extreme skiing, racers on the World Cup tour ski challenging conditions on various mountains. That's where most of the comparisons end.

The snow on World Cup race courses is injected with chemicals that turn it into a tilted ribbon of ice. The terrain varies from steep to shallow and undulates throughout the course. It often includes side hills and fall away turns, steep tilts to the left or right of skiers' direction of travel.

Gates dictate where racers will turn and require turns of different radiuses and lengths. The courses are unpredictable, set at the whims of whichever coach drew the short straw that day.

Ruts and moguls form. Larger knolls can launch skiers skyward for the length of a football field. Speeds in super-G and downhill are intended to frighten racers with the possibility of life-threatening injuries…and, tragically, some racers are hurt badly in these disciplines.

There are compressions where skiers traveling downhill at 70 miles per hour or more are suddenly squashed by an uphill wall of snow. If they can stand up, they will usually be required make a high speed turn while bearing g forces that feel like 500 pounds on their backs.

In World Cup racing, there are no style points. The winners are determined by the cold electric eye of a clock that counts thousandths of a second.

(Ok, now write your note about who are better skiers than World Cup racers.)

So, when you take even a look at what the best skiers in the world do, you'll see a nearly complete disregard for whether their skis are jammed together.

Google images of World Cup ski racers in action. You'll quickly see that their skis almost never touch. In fact, you'll see a variety of skills they use to scramble down the fastest line through the gates. These include parallel turns, diverging step turns, turns started or finished on the "wrong" ski and even wedge turns.

Yes, *wedge* turns.

When skiers ask me for tips today, I usually respond by saying something about being flattered that they asked me. (This is false modesty on my part. I know I wear my irreproachable skiing awesomeness like a cloak that's visible to all around me.) I usually say, kidding aside, that I don't know what they could do to improve in their skiing.

This evokes their thoughts about what they want to learn. Usually, it's how to ski moguls better. That seems to be another universal desire among skiers.

Teaching someone successfully takes all the steps I describe in the previous chapter. It's a one hour commitment on my part and my student's. Most people who ask for ski tips are good hearted, but really don't want to focus on skill-building for an hour. So, usually I'll make a couple of suggestions on the lift and move on. Once we get to the top, let's ski and have fun!

This was one of the longest chapters in this book. Why? Because discussions of "how to ski" are universally viewed as foreplay for those seeking skier's nirvana. And, as you can tell, I subscribe to a complementary approach to authors of books on ski technique: play with your skis, have fun, expand your repertoire, relax, enjoy your ski vacation.

# 14

# CHOOSING SKI RESORTS:
# SIZE MATTERS

Your partner for achieving ecstasy on ski holidays is the ski resort itself. Choose a resort too small and you'll go unsatisfied. Choose a resort too big and it won't fit either.

I just love metaphors.

*Vertical drop* is calculated by the altitude at the top of the resort minus the altitude at the bottom. You can usually find the altitudes of the top and bottom of a mountain on the resort's website or trail map. Vertical drop is one of the best indicators of what it's going to feel like to ski there.

If you're an expert skier, in great shape, 26 years old and you like long runs, a resort where the top of the mountain is at 2,000 feet and the bottom is at 1,700 isn't going to please you. That's 300 feet of vertical.

You'll have about enough mountain to tease yourself with six turns on each run. Then, you'll have to wait on the lift line and ride back to the top. About 5% of your time will be spent skiing. You'll go postal.

On the other hand, if you're a 48 year old, out of shape beginner, you don't need a mountain with 3,000 feet of vertical drop either. You're only going to see the bottom 200 feet of the mountain where the bunny hill is…and maybe a few restaurants and shops near the base lodge.

Then, there are cost considerations related to vertical drop. Most 3,000-foot-high resorts are located where there are no people, only elk. You might have to fly or drive a long way to get there. That could easily add $500 US to the cost of your ski holiday.

So, what about most of us skiers who are between solid intermediate and expert skiers? We are a large chunk of the skiing population. What size resort should we be choosing? I have the answer.

It's the "Rule of the 500s."

Take the number of days you'll be skiing at your holiday destination. Multiply the number of days by 500. That will give you the suggested minimum vertical drop for the resort you should ski.

So, let's say, you're just going to ski for one day. In most cases, a resort with (1 day x 500 =) 500 vertical feet, will keep you entertained for a day. It might even be large enough to keep you happy for two days, but not much more.

If you're taking three or four days, look for a resort closer to (4 x 500) or a vertical drop of 2,000 feet.

If you going to be skiing for five or six days, then you're definitely a candidate for (6 x 500) or about 3,000 feet of vertical. You don't have to limit yourself to looking for 3,000 feet of vertical.

The Law of 500s is a just one guide for choosing ski resorts, depending on how many days you plan to ski on your vacation.

What if you'll have access to multiple resorts? Then you can violate the Law of 500s. It's no longer a misdemeanor to go under the minimum vertical drop.

Multiple resorts are often within several minutes of each other. This is fairly common in mountain resort areas. And some "short" ski resorts, those under 1,000 feet of vertical, are spread out across several mountains. So, there's plenty of variability in the terrain to keep you entertained.

# 15

# 4 MILLION WAYS
# TO SAVE ON LIFT PASSES

For most of us, the size of our wallets matters as much as the size of the ski resort. With single day lift passes exceeding $100 at some US resorts. and similar high prices in other parts of ski world, it pays to check into ways to save money on lift tickets.

If you're a beginner, and especially if you're a school student, this is easy. Many local ski resorts offer learn-to-ski programs to surrounding schools. If your school doesn't have a program, look for resorts that offer discounted or free beginner packages for ski rentals, lift tickets and lessons. To find these programs, just type into your favorite search engine, "ski resorts near me."

If you're not a student, but want to start skiing economically, look into small resorts. These often have vertical drops of 1000 feet or less. (Review chapter 14 to learn how to choose ski resorts.) Smaller resorts charge a lot less for lift tickets than larger ones. They provide perfect, intimate settings for you to take your first lessons and get used to using ski equipment.

For the rest of us experienced skiers, there are other ways to save. If you happen to have a favorite resort and will be skiing or snowboarding there often, it may be worthwhile to buy a season pass. Check the websites of your favorite ski resorts. The best deals on season passes are offered months before ski season begins.

If you're planning to spread your ski-ventures across several resorts, check into discount multi-resort passes online. Simply Google "multiple ski resort discounts". In the U.S., we get more than four million search results. A growing number of resorts are cooperating to promote a richer array of skiing options with one heavily discounted pass.

Lift line waits can get long, extending beyond 15 or 30 minutes at some heavily discounted resorts. Sometimes it pays to check skier discussions on social media to find out when and at what resorts the lift lines are shorter.

Then, there are group discounts. If you can wrangle twenty friends or ski club members to join you for a day of skiing, many resorts will give you an attractive group rate.

So far in our journey, we've covered how to become a smarter buyer of ski industry products and services. We've figured out what kinds of skis, ski boots and skiwear meet your personal skiing preferences. By this point in this book, you know what's behind all the fancy ski industry labeling and can find the best deals on all that stuff. You've learned whether to rent, demo or buy skis. You've even learned how to get yourself and all your ski equipment to and from ski resorts economically and safely.

You could save hundreds of dollars (or euros, yen or whatever your country's currency) just by following any one of the tips we've covered. Is this a great book, or what? I can hardly believe people can buy this book for less than the price of three cups of coffee (or if you're at a ski resort, one cup of coffee.) And, we're not even finished yet.

In the next chapter we'll talk about another big skiing expense—lodging. And, if you've ever gone on holiday with another person, you know lodging decisions are never simple especially if you're planning a romantic getaway. Double the complexity if children are involved. So the next chapter will not only help you save money, but also help you save your relationships.

Wow, what a book, huh?

# 16

# LODGING, CHILDREN AND THE
# POSSIBILITY OF ROMANCE

Lodging first. You have two choices. You can stay at the resort for the luxury and convenience it gives you or pay about half as much to stay in a place about 15 minutes to an hour's drive from the resort.

That's it.

What will influence which lodging is right for you? Children and whether or not you're counting on a romantic interlude with your significant other or spouse.

I'm opposed to taking children skiing for the first time before they can carry a pair of skis, drive and maybe even hold a job. Before I get into the reasons, let me invite you to check out hundreds of low-cost learn-to-ski programs for children in the U.S. and other countries. The kids are supervised, bussed to local resorts after school, get rental equipment, ski lessons and lift passes and then bussed home. Millions of kids become happy skiers and snowboarders this way. Best of all, there's no wear and tear on their parents.

But, if you're considering taking your young child to a ski resort for their first time, I have two pieces of advice.

Number one: No parent should take a kid skiing before mine did. I was 15. I was deprived of skiing for years and look what a model citizen I've become as a result. Deprivation builds character.

Instead of starting your kids skiing, return home from a long ski weekend with tan faces and that telltale, post-ski weekend afterglow. Tell your kids about the great time you had. They will want to go skiing with you next time. But, they can't unless they get at least four As and nothing below a B on their next report cards. And, oh, they have to volunteer once a week at a homeless shelter.

Number two: If you bring young kids to their first ski resort experience, they will suck the life out of you. You'll be carrying three pairs of skis instead of one and running between child care, your guest room, ski school, the lifts and the bathroom. If you're lucky, you might ski for two hours each day.

Don't wimp out, skier. You got this book because you're a diehard skier, or you aspire to be. At the very least, when you go skiing, you should be on holiday. You can be Super Dad or Super Mom, provider and protector the other 363 days a year.

So, how do young children influence where you'll bed down for the night on ski vacations? Your spouse, or whoever's loins from which the little ones sprang, gets the majority vote on where you're going to stay.

She, or he as the case may be, has expectations about your being a good sport. Being a good sport includes doing what's best for the kids, right? That could mean finding the most convenient accommodations on the mountain. Like that ski-in ski-out condo that costs $800 US per night. You know, the one with the hot tub that someone's kids dumped laundry detergent into last year. Oh, wasn't that great fun? Let's go back!

Don't take young kids skiing for the first time, especially if your ski weekend is with your ski buddies or girlfriend, boyfriend or spouse. I'm not saying you wouldn't derive joy from watching your little darlings slide gleefully down the hill. But, if *you* actually want to ski and bond with other adults, don't bring your kids! You'd have a better chance of skiing if you snorted flu virus the week before your ski trip.

Besides, doing what's best for the kids includes teaching them character. In most of the civilized world, with the possible exception of Dubai, depriving children of an expensive ski holidays is not considered abuse. So, you don't have to feel guilty about this. You can actually dangle ski holidays like carrots before their flaring nostrils as rewards for good behavior.

So, your adult ski holiday partners will influence where you stay. This might have special significance if you intend to extend the entertainment portion of your day late into the evening, maybe with your spouse or significant other while on the trip.

Sure, you should never go to bed angry. But, if one of you has brought little ones along, you're going to stay wherever it makes that parent happy. That's because it's unwise to upset your potential bedmate before the ski holiday even begins.

So, you can see how where you stay is going to be influenced by the presence of children…and potential for a little romance.

Now, if you happen to be a child whose parents are paying for you to ski or snowboard, congratulations. You are among a lucky few, not just because you can ski, but because you also have incredibly generous parents. In return, you should plan to support them when they retire at age forty.

# 17

# FIRST TIME SKIING? THE 5 STEP GUIDE TO HAVING A GREAT DAY

If you're curious about trying skiing for the first time, this chapter is just for you my adventurous friend. There's lots of information in previous chapters that you'll find useful. We'll cover additional tips about how to get ready for your first trip to the slopes.

Let me be the first to welcome you to the "dark side". You'll soon see why most skiers and snowboarders are fanatics about these wonderful sports. There are lots of reasons—the thrills of skiing, incredible scenery and many social aspects.

We love introducing newbies to our sport. So, if you don't know anyone who skis, joining a local ski club will put you in touch with dozens of friendly people.

If you don't have time to join a ski club or are shy, you still don't have to go it alone. Your buddy, Dan, is here to help you have a ski-tatstic start to your ski adventures.

In this chapter, I'll make a few assumptions. The first is that you're going solo on your very first ski day. Unlike many skiers who were introduced to the sport through a parent or friend, it's just you and me…in your head…going on your first ski trip. I'll try to be as informative as possible.

The second assumption is that, even if you know a skier or two, they're *sadists*. They'll bring you to the top of the mountain and push you off the edge—just for their own entertainment.

Hey, I know I'm prejudging your friends. But, this scenario has occurred often enough for me to evoke some productive paranoia on your part.

Here's where I'm headed with this…

*Don't let a friend try to teach you how to ski.* Take a lesson from a an instructor. You'll be happier, safer and skiing better, sooner.

Also, ask an instructor or a lift attendant to help you get on a ski lift for the first time. If you have any doubts about my infinite wisdom on this, reread chapter 12, "Six Skiing Tips that Every Amateur Instructor Shares."

I also assume that you're in reasonably good shape, whatever your age. You can climb a few flights of stairs and get up easily from sitting on the floor. You'll need to be fit enough to stand, ski and get up from falls. Falling in snow is a natural part of skiing. (I used to have my beginner ski school students grade each other's falls. Awards given at the end of the lesson.) You and your doctor should have an understanding of your physical conditioning, which permits you to ski.

So, let's start preparing for your first *fantastic* day on the hill.

*Choose a Ski Resort*

You need not find a large expensive ski resort. You'll be getting your ski legs in the beginners' area at the bottom of a ski hill. So, no use in buying access to a massive three-thousand-foot-tall mountain. An inexpensive, local ski resort will do perfectly.

Your only requirements are a resort that has snow, a rental shop where you can rent skis and ski boots, a ski school and a base lodge where you can relax, get some nourishment and enjoy the mountain scenery. Most small ski resorts typically have everything you'll need.

Some resorts have to learn-to-ski days where you can rent equipment and take beginner lessons for little or no cost. These days are rare, but it's worth Googling local beginner ski days to figure out when they'll be happening.

*Dress for the Cold*

We'll keep clothing costs to a minimum. Read chapter 8 to learn about the layers of clothing that will help you stay warm and happy. The nice thing about layers is you can take layers off or put them on as your comfort dictates.

You don't need to spend a lot of money on a matching ski jacket and pants either. You basically need protection from the wind and snow on your outermost layer, your shell, which traps warm air inside your insulating layers.

I've sometimes used inexpensive nylon jackets and nylon warm up pants as my outermost layer. The baggier, the better. That way I can easily fit my insulating layers underneath, usually polyester fleece sweatpants and tops, and still have enough room to move around. I'm perfectly warm and comfortable.

Now, let's take care of your noggin. You'll need a thick winter hat that pulls down over your ears (or a ski helmet) and eye protection from the sun, wind and snow. You don't have to lay out a hundred bucks for ski goggles, but at the very least you should wear sunglasses, ideally the wrap-around kind.

I also recommend getting a fleece neck gaiter. You can pull the top of the gaiter up over your face if it's a very cold day and stuff it in your pocket if it's warm.

Fingers and toes are always the body parts that get cold first if any part gets cold at all. Water-resistant insulated mittens are best for keeping fingers warm. Insulated gloves (not your thin leather driving gloves, Sparky) will do. You can also carry a thin pair of glove liners in your pocket for extra insulation if your fingers get cold.

Buy a pair of ski socks. Ski socks are made of special fabrics that keep your toes warm and dry. They're thinner than you might expect of a winter sock. That's so your feet can slide easily into ski boots and you still have insulating bubbles of warm air in the boots' toe boxes.

You can find everything you need at most ski shops. If there isn't a shop near you, try shopping online.

*Get to the Resort*

It's almost always better traveling into ski country with a companion. You can share your adventure on the road, on the mountain and in the base lodge. In the unlikely event that one of you needs help, your travel partner can provide aid or alert ski patrol.

Leave plenty of time to get to the resort especially if roads are snowy. You'll want to arrive at least one hour before your ski lesson. Check in advance for when the resort conducts beginner ski lessons. Alternatively, you can arrange for a slightly more expensive private lesson that's scheduled whenever convenient for you.

*Gear Up for Fun*

Once you've parked your car, get out, stretch and take in the mountain scenery. You're in ski country!

Collect your gear (in the daypack I talked about in chapter 11) and head toward the base lodge. No need to put all your warm weather clothes on yet. Just put on your insulating layers, ski socks and whatever else you need to stay warm as you walk to the lodge.

We've got to pay for the day and get your rental equipment before we put on your outer shells, hat, mittens, eye protection and gaiter.

When you get to the base lodge look for the ticket windows. Let the ticket attendant know that you're a beginner skier who needs to rent ski equipment and take a lesson. Sometimes a resort will include a lift ticket in its beginner package.

You'll be asked to fill out a ski rental form that asks for your height, weight and skiing ability. No fudging here! This information is used by the rental shop to choose the right length skis and set the release settings on your skis' bindings.

The binding releases your foot in a fall to reduce the risk of injury.

When you get your skis and boots, you'll be ready to get fully dressed for your first day on the slopes. Most resorts have lockers where you can store your gear. At smaller resorts, skiers often store their day packs in the base lodge cafeteria. Take your wallet, keys and other valuables with you and keep them in jacket and pants pockets that zip closed.

Just before your ski lesson, put your ski boots, jacket, hat and mittens on. When you're all set, carry your skis outside onto the snow where you'll join your instructor.

Congratulations! You're about to become a skier!

*Stay Fueled and Hydrated*

Beginners often underestimate how much energy they'll burn while skiing. Your first lesson will last 60 to 90 minutes. It's normal after a lesson to want to sit down, relax and enjoy a snack and some juice or hot cocoa. You've had an adventurous morning!

Make sure to keep yourself hydrated, especially if the resort is more than five thousand feet above sea level. Dehydration up there can spur altitude sickness and a nasty headache. Stay away from alcoholic drinks until the end of your ski day, if you partake at all.

After your lesson, you can continue skiing as much as you want until the resort closes. That's usually around 4 pm. Enjoy!

# 18

# 10 TYPES OF SNOW AND
# WHERE YOU'LL FIND THEM

All ski resorts have snow. But, if you had to choose where to ski and snowboard just on the basis of snow types, you could. Each provides a unique skiing experience. You'll find different snow types under different weather conditions and at different points in the ski season.

There are actually dozens of words to describe snow conditions among skiing cultures worldwide. Most relate in some way to the following ten.

*Champagne powder* – Bottomless, light airy snow that billows up and sometimes over the heads of skiers as they blast down a slope. It's so dry that it almost doesn't qualify as precipitation. Champagne powder is found in the high altitude mountain environments that are inland, far away from moisturizing lakes and oceans. Utah, USA, for example is 700 miles from the nearest ocean and rightly boasts of its champagne powder.

*Powder* – Powder in all its forms is prized by advanced and expert skiers. That doesn't mean that it's the easiest stuff to ski. That's because you're floating *through* the snow and not skiing *on* the snow. Unless you stand with roughly equal weight on both skis and turn them at the same time, one ski can rise to the surface while the other dives to the bottom, which means you're going to do some tumbling. Furthermore, you can't see or hear your skis, something that skiers accustomed to skiing on hard pack can find discomforting.

Depending on weather conditions, powder can increase in density, moisture and weight within hours or days of falling. The coldest, shaded portions of mountains will store the lighter, fluffy kind of powder. The sunlit and more heavily skied slopes feature heavier snow. These variations in density are what makes powder one of the most interesting and fun challenges for skiers. Each mountain has a different shape, sun exposure and personality that really comes out on powder days.

*Packed powder* – Also known as *ego snow, corduroy, groomed* or *cruisers*, these are the snow surfaces that are fluffed, flattened and finished to pristine skiable surfaces nearly every day at most resorts.

*Sierra cement* – This is the wet, heavy powder that falls in the Sierra, located between California and Nevada USA, and other ski resorts worldwide that are humidified by nearby oceans and large lakes. This could have been champagne powder but for the fact that this snow falls in clumps consisting of dozens of moist flakes. It can be bottomless and does qualify as powder in its own right. However, Sierra cement compresses under its own weight. Skiing through it requires a more strength, momentum and skill than you would need for most hard pack skiing.

*Windblown* –Like Sierra cement, but usually not as moist, windblown snow has been subjected to winds literally pushing down on it. Think of it as a dense powder. Unlike champagne powder in which skiers can sink chest deep when skiing through it, windblown snow compresses quickly and provides a lot of flotation.

*Breakable crust* – When the top layer of snow has thawed and refrozen, creating an thin crust over the lighter powder beneath, this is breakable crust. At least, you hope it's breakable.

*Crud* – Crud is like a box of chocolates—you never know what you're going to get. Crud is what remains after multiple skiers have skied a powdery slope. There are ski tracks going in all directions. There are piles of heavy powder that will slow your skis and voids where your skis suddenly accelerate. The challenges of skiing crud increase as the snow becomes more moist, dense or goes through freeze-thaw cycles. With crud, you have to be ready for anything…because *everything* is out there on the hill. Windblown, crust and crud are more typically found at resorts with significant off-trail ski terrain.

*Ice* – Ice is also widely known as *bullet proof*. There's some disagreement about what constitutes ice on a ski hill. Having skied in New England USA, where Nor'easters can bring winter thaws, rain and then refreeze, I've seen real ice—the kind that's transparent and has bubbles in it. Chip it and you've got a cube for your martini. This compares with what most skiers call icy slopes, which are just slopes that have hard surfaces of very firm, compressed snow. It's noisy when our edges go across it. But, unlike the cocktail ingredient, you can still turn on it. Most World Cup race courses are set on hard, icy snow.

*Corn* – Corn is a coarse granular wet snow that skiers find mostly in Spring. It's the result of tiny snow pellets melting during the day followed by refreezing at night. In the cold mornings, corn is a frozen granular surface. It can sound and feel scratchy until later in the day when it warms up and the snow pellets separate. Then, corn can be especially fun. If you happen to be skiing bumps, corn has a way of flinging upward as you blast through piles of it.

*Snirt* – This is just like it sounds, a combination of snow and dirt. Snirt is found in the Spring when dirt and pollen that has fallen all season is concentrated in the remaining snow pack. The effect is grey, dirty snow. The dirty stuff sticks to the wax on the bottoms of your skis, so take care to clean them after a day of snirt skiing.

Generally speaking, you'll experience the widest variety of snow conditions at resorts with larger temperature differences between their peaks and bases, and where you'll find snow in sun, shade, above and below the tree line. Snow making and grooming assure fun skiing at most ski resorts regardless of location.

# 19

# FALLING FUN

Skiers and snowboarders have aversions to falling. I can't say falling is my favorite skiing experience but since it's inevitable, best to find the humor in it. Most of my best falls were pretty hilarious. Only a few were embarrassing, particularly when I was wearing a ski instructor's jacket.

Like most instructors, I aspired to be a paragon of skiing athleticism and grace. So, when yours truly came screaming down a recently cut cat track cut so deep and narrow I couldn't throw my skis sideways to slow down, I knew my flying wedge was only a warm up to the spectacle to come for skiers waiting in the lift queue. The cat track ended with a high berm and so too did the forward movement of my feet. If anyone had missed the preliminaries, the *click-click* of my bindings flying opening and audible thud of my faceplant caught their attention and applause. I did what any self-respecting entertainer does. I took a bow.

The unavoidable fact is if you enjoy sliding down mountains with boards stuck to your feet, you won't be upright on them all the time. We all fall, even the experts, even the best skiers in the world.

Beginner skiers are usually afraid of falling. They usually associate falling with broken legs. But, when I assure beginners that their ski bindings will release in a fall, vastly reducing the possibility of injuries, their focus turns to how they'll look. Everyone wants to look like they know what they're doing. Beginners need reassurance that other skiers won't look down on them.

That's when I'd ask beginners this question. What's the difference between how beginning skiers fall and how expert skiers fall? This always evoked expressions of bewilderment, like I'd just given a pop quiz. The tension disappeared when I gave them the answer: Speed.

When a beginner falls, it's at four miles an hour. When an expert falls, it's sometimes at forty miles an hour. It looks like a comet streaking down the hill. Helmets and boots poke through the mist in rotation. Skis, googles and hats are strewn down the piste. Skiers call that a garage sale. Trust me, when experts fall, it's funnier.

You're going to fall. We all fall. Falling isn't failing. It's just part of the fun.

To learn how to ski and snowboard—and get back up when you fall—take a few lessons and enjoy playing in the snow. Skiing and snowboarding are actually reasonably safe sports if you follow the Alpine (or Skiers) Responsibility Code, which is displayed at every ski area.

The rules of the code are pretty common sensical. There are ten rules. Here are my top four. Ski in control. Yield to skiers ahead of you. *They* have the right of way. Stop on the side of the trail out of the way of other skiers. Look up hill for approaching skiers before starting again or crossing trails.

So, there it is. We're at the end of this updated edition of the *Skier's Gift Book that's Sweeping the Globe (Sort of)*. You now know how to find the skis, boots, skiwear, friends, ski resorts, snow and methods of transport get to and from the slopes in style. Thanks for taking this extended lift ride with me.

Have a good run!

## ABOUT THE AUTHOR

Dan Cody is a writer, speaker and advocate for all things snow. He has worked as a ski resort marketing manager, ski instructor, ski education program manager, resort hotel manager, ski shop salesperson and ski tour leader. In addition to authoring two editions of *The Skiers Gift Book that's Sweeping the Globe (Sort of)*, Dan leads a five-session dry-land ski technique workshop that emphasizes fun and complements on-snow instruction.

Dan enjoys cycling, hiking, playing jazz and exploring the world. His most recent expedition was in Egypt.

To arrange for Dan to contribute to your blog, speak at your event or lead a workshop, email him at DanCodyAuthor@gmail.com.